I0393606

LeadWell™

*The World's Finest
Leadership Training Curriculum
For 14-23 Year Olds*

Ruby Training Module
Leader Workbook

⚶ SUCCESS™
Leadership Project Plan

Copyright-Licensing-Use

This project manual is part of the **Lead**Well. Training curriculum, along with the book:

The content of this Project Manual is copyrighted by Alan E. Nelson, EdD., ©2013, 2017, 2021. Use it with the **Lead**Well. training curriculum, created by **Lead**Young Training Systems. It is unlawful to copy any part of this manual. For more info, contact us at at the website below.

ISBN-13: 978-1479198115
ISBN-10: 1479198110

Table of Contents

LeadYoung Training Systems © 2013, 2017, 2021 LeadWell Ruby Module
www.LeadYoungTraining.com

A letter from the founder of LeadYoung Training Systems

Dear Young Leader:

I'm so impressed that you've chosen to be involved in this executive-caliber training program called **Lead**Well. I want to apologize to you that so many older adults tend to take your leadership ability lightly and frequently overlook teens and young adults as potentially strong leaders. I've discovered that the significant difference between leaders like you and those running large organizations is experience.

That's what we want to help you get in this training program, experience. You'll be doing several project-based activities where you'll take turns leading your peers, receiving feedback, as well as discussing what happened. You'll also be a part of an executive team, planning a project that you'll actually implement. This is real world opportunity to gain experience as well.

In addition, you'll be reading portions of the **Lead**Well book. I'd encourage you to read **Lead**Young. The book is unique in that it was written from the perspective of things that young leaders face, helping you get ahead. Both are designed for 14- to 23-year-olds, based on your unique experiences and stage in life.

I have to admit, I didn't always think young people could lead effectively. But I was wrong. I'm convinced they can. Leading isn't for everyone, but if it's for you, then this program will help you develop your potential. Have fun, learn a lot, and please keep in touch with us. We want to hear what you learned from this program and how we can improve it for others like you around the world.

Yours truly,

Alan E. Nelson, EdD
Founder

4 Core Leadership Concepts in the Ruby Module

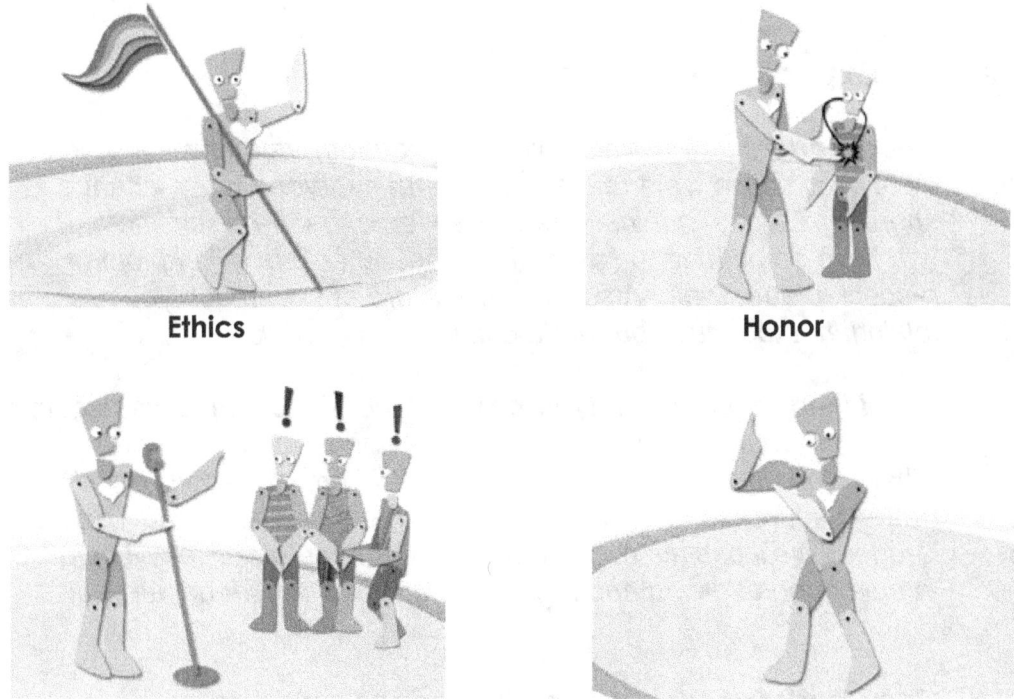

Ethics	**Honor**
Communication	**Power**

Here are some things to consider during these meetings:

Ethics: How does a leader decide what is right, even when the answers aren't always clear? What can a leader do to avoid lying, stealing, cheating, and other actions that hurt the team in the long run?

Honor: How does a leader respect people, even when they may not perform as needed or have a bad attitude? What are practical ways that leaders can help people know they are valuable, treating them with dignity?

Communication: How can a leader be effective in speaking and writing? Why does a leader need to know how to listen well? Why is it important for the team to communicate if it is to function effectively?

Power: How can a leader obtain influence, even if s/he is young and does not have a formal position of authority? What are the multiple sources of power, and how can young leaders tap into them?

LeadWell. Ruby Module

Training Expectations:

1. ***Good leaders listen well***. *We learn from others and we also learn by talking, so we want to make sure that everyone has a chance to share their ideas, not just a few. Leaders must be disciplined. If you have something to say while someone else is talking, out of respect, please wait. Also try to be aware of how much you're talking; not too much but not too little.*

2. ***Good leaders continually improve***. *One of the things we're going work on in **Lead**Well is giving and receiving feedback from each other. You and your Koach will continually provide short, Good-Better-Best responses to you after you have served as the Team Leader. We'll explain this in a moment, but the practice will help you be good at giving and receiving improvement ideas, all your life.*

3. ***Good leaders honor others***. *What you say and how you treat team members is very important in leading. Therefore, we will not tolerate negativity, teasing, making fun of others, or doing anything meant to intimidate or hurt others. This is a safe place. We all like to learn where we feel like we're respected and liked.*

4. ***Good leaders can follow, too***. *If you don't know how to be a good follower, you won't be a very good leader. Your Trainer and Koaches and are here to facilitate your learning, so we want you to respect our roles. But when one of your colleagues is leading your team, please respond like a good team member.*

5. ***Good leaders are responsible.*** *Please bring this workbook to every session and the **Lead**Well book when assigned. Please be on time and try to avoid leaving early. If you'll be gone or late, let us know ahead of time. Sometimes you'll have responsibilities to fulfill between meetings, so if you do, we expect you to follow through and come prepared.*

‫כ Team Leader Feedback

One of the most important things you can learn as a leader is to give and receive feedback that is effective. This will allow you to continue to grow and improve, all of your life. A big failure of leaders is that they often offend people in how they confront issues that need to be corrected and they do not give feedback in a way that people receive it well.

A bigger failure of leaders is that they often reduce valuable feedback because they are insecure, become defensive, and intimidate people to the point that they are unwilling to provide information to improve leadership or the task. Therefore, **Lead**Well has you give and receive peer feedback on a regular basis, along with reviewing your own performance when you are the Team Leader. At first this may take a little extra effort, but after a while, it will become second nature to you.

The following page provides an array of questions that you consider when you are providing the short feedback forms that you'll be doing. Generally, the Trainer or Koach will assign 1 team member to do a GBB (Good-Better-Best) Feedback form on the Team Leader per activity and 2 team members while leading the SUCCESS meetings.

Great leaders get feedback and are self-aware. The Leader Self-Awareness sheet is a quick way for you to do this as well. Good leaders ask for feedback. After each Training Session, you'll have about 1 minute to write about your own leading, went well and what could be made even better next time. Try to be specific, short, and print so others can read your writing.

3 Points for Great Feedback:

1. **Be aware**. Providing quality feedback will be difficult if you're not paying attention to what the Team Leader is doing and how the team is responding. Prepare to provide feedback, meaning you'll need to stay engage and alert.

2. **Keep the feedback constructive.** Be positive and focus on what went well and what could be done next time. Effective feedback is information that is usable. If you make someone made by being offensive, that information will not be used.

3. **Try to be specific**. "You did a good job" isn't very helpful. Try to be specific. "When you asked Ben for his idea, you made him feel included and I noticed he got more involved at that point. Good."

Receiving good feedback is important as well. If you have questions, go over the responses with your Koach or Trainer who may provide extra insight. Remember, this is about growing and getting better, so embrace the feedback, even if it feels embarrassing or awkward at the moment. People need various things from their leaders.

2 Ideas for Leader Feedback

Here are a few things to consider when you are observing another person leading. These are ideas to help you provide specific comments on the Team Leader Feedback note:

Team

___ 1. How did the leader communicate with team members?

___ 2. How did the leader do in providing clear directions?

___ 3. How did the leader affirm us during the activity?

___ 4. How did the leader handle conflict on the team?

___ 5. How did the leader listen, gather ideas and input from the team?

___ 6. How did the leader help people match task roles with theirs strengths?

___ 7. How well did the leader stay primarily focused on the team vs. the task?

Task

___ 1. How did the leader help the team strategize toward the goal?

___ 2. How did the leader help us stay on task as a team?

___ 3. How did the leader keep us aware of the time and limited resources?

___ 4. How did the leader help us improve, re-strategize and get better?

___ 5. How did the leader assist the team in problem solving?

___ 6. How did the leading provided affect the outcome of the task?

___ 7. Was the balance too task oriented, too people oriented or just right?

Style/Summary

___ 1. Was the primary style Tell, Sell, Gel or Del? Did it fit the situation?

___ 2. What else specifically could help the leader improve next time?

Good-Better-Best (GBB) Feedback Form

The primary communication tool that you'll use for giving feedback to your Team Leaders (and that you'll be receiving after you're the Team Leader) is the GBB Feedback form.

The purpose of this card is to provide written feedback to a Team Leader on how s/he led. Put the Team Leader's name on the top left space and your name as the Responder. Be sure to print or write so it can be read.

The reason we use the A+ symbol is because we want the A-quality feedback to help use become A+ leaders, who are constantly learning and improving. Therefore, even though there should be one item where we might improve and/or lead differently, this is a positive, not a negative. Good feedback doesn't tell us what we did wrong, but helps us know how we can get better.

You want to share 3 (and only 3) items on each GBB:

Good: The first question you answer is, "What is 1 thing the Team Leader did well (good)?" Try to be specific and limit it to 1 thing.

Better: The second question you answer is, "What is 1 thing the Team Leader might do to be even better next time?" This may be something to improve on, either from your perspective as a team member or merely another idea. Even if the Team Leader did well, we can always improve, so perhaps share an additional idea. Again, the focus is on "next time" since none of us can undo what we've already done. Limit this to 1 thing.

Best: The third question you answer is, "What is the 1 thing you think the Team Leader did best?" Again, be specific, but you want to leave the Team Leader with a positive compliment. Limit it to 1 thing.

You may or may not be asked to share this out loud. Either way, it is something the Team Leader can take home and review later. Plus, it helps you as a leader to think of how to improve your own leadership as you analyze what it is like to be led by others.

Example of Poor Feedback:

> **Leader's Name** ___Jesse_____   **Responder's Name** _____ Susie_____
>
> **1 thing you did well was:** *You helped us work together.*
>
> **1 thing that would help me, our team or another idea for next time is:** *You didn't use your time well. You should have kept us going faster.*
>
> **1 thing you did <u>great</u> was:** *You did a good job.*

Example of Good Feedback:

> **Leader's Name** ___Jesse_____   **Responder's Name** _____ Susie_____
>
> **1 thing you did well was:** *We only had 1 minute to prepare, so you immediately gave us directions on what each of us should do.*
>
> **1 thing that would help me, our team or another idea for next time is:** *Even if you only have a little time, perhaps ask for 2-3 quick suggestions from people, so we feel like you listened to us a bit.*
>
> **1 thing you did <u>great</u> was:** *When we kept dropping the ball, you noticed it and changed who was throwing and who was catching. Good improvement.*

ʔ Leader Self-Awareness

Here are a few things to consider as you reflect upon your leading as the Team Leader. Mark 3-5 you felt you did most effectively with an **X** and 2-3 you want to improve on next time with an **O**, (if they fit the situation).

Team

____ 1. I communicated well with team members.

____ 2. I clarified the task and the directions were clear.

____ 3. I affirmed the team members during and after the activity.

____ 4. I handled conflict well among the team members.

____ 5. I listened, gathered ideas and effectively used feedback from the team.

____ 6. I helped people find roles that seemed to best match their strengths.

____ 7. I kept my primary attention on the function of the team more than the task.

Task

____ 1. I effectively assisted the team in strategizing toward the goal?

____ 2. I was effective in keep the team focused on the task.

____ 3. I kept our team aware of the time and other limited resources?

____ 4. I effectively helped the team improve, re-strategize, and get better?

____ 5. I assisted the team in problem solving when we seemed to get stuck.

Style/Summary

____ 1. I maintained a good balance between task and people.

____ 2. My primary style was Tell, Sell, Gel or Del (circle 1). Did it fit the "sitch?"

____ 3. What else specifically could I do next time to improve my leading? (Write)

LeadWell. Ruby Module
Session #1: Ethics (Values)

 Key Concept: Great leading does what is right, to make the world better.

Activity #1: *Ethical Drama:* Leaders recognize ethical situations and the importance of decisions. In this activity, we created and performed mini-dramas, providing right and wrong choice options.

Activity #2: *Inverted Pyramid:* Leaders are tempted to make unethical decisions under the stress of competition. In this activity, one or more teams broke the rules during an activity, to help us discuss how and why this happens in real life.

Peak Performance Assignment: Read Chapter 1 (pages 9-14) in your book, **Lead**Well, and prepare to discuss the questions at the end of the chapter.

Leader Reflection: One thing I learned from this training meeting:

LeadYoung. Training Systems © 2013, 2017, 2021 LeadWell Ruby Module
www.LeadYoungTraining.com

LeadWell. Ruby Module
Session #2: Ethics (Values)

 Key Concept: Great leading does what is right, to make the world better.

L.E.A.D. Activity #1: *The Situation:* Leaders have to make decisions that are not always clear-cut. Ethical situations are not always easy and risk some type of loss either way.

Peak Performance Assignment: What's one thing you got out of your discussion of the **Lead**Well book?

L.E.A.D. Activity #2: *Go For It:* Leaders are responsible for helping their teams & organizations to know and play by the rules. When they don't, the team can suffer.

Notes: One thing I learned from this training session:

LeadWell. Ruby Module
Session #3: Honor (Attitudes)

 Key Concept: Great leading values people, to give them dignity.

Activity #1: *The Wrap:* Leaders practice a variety of honoring things they can say and write to others. Plus, they "wrap" their conversations with words that express respect and dignity, even when they disagree with others.

Activity #2: *Introducing:* Leaders practice introducing people to each other in order to honor them publicly. They are also careful to avoid using humor that might unintentionally dishonor or embarrass people.

Peak Performance Assignment: Read Chapter 5 on Honor (pages 35-42) in **Lead**Well and respond to the questions.

Notes: One thing I learned from this training meeting:

LeadWell. Ruby Module
Session #4: Honor (Attitudes)

 Key Concept: Great leading values people, to give them dignity.

L.E.A.D. Activity #1: *Cheer Leading:* Leaders frequently work with limited resources and must assist teams in maximizing these resources, while not alienating people who have creative ideas.

Peak Performance Assignment: What's one thing you got out of your discussion of the **Lead**Well book?

L.E.A.D. Activity #2: *Thanks Giving:* Leaders continually honor people by expressing appreciation for what they do, making sure not to overlook common tasks as well as great productivity. They write lots of notes.

Notes: One thing I learned from this training session:

LeadWell Ruby Module
Session #5: Communication (Relationships)

 Key Concept: Great leading gets the point across, to be clear.

L.E.A.D. Activity #1: *Speed Speech:* Leaders often need to come up with presentations quickly. Creating a strong message and visual aid are important to effectively getting a point across to others.

L.E.A.D. Activity #2: *Clues:* Leaders are primarily responsible for making sure their teams have adequate information to accomplish tasks. When teams don't have sufficient info, they are less likely to achieve the goal or do it with confidence.

Peak Performance Assignment: Read Chapter 11 on Communication (pages 85-92) in **Lead**Well and respond to the questions.

Notes: One thing I learned from this training meeting:

LeadWell. Ruby Module
Session #6: **Communication** (Relationships)

 Key Concept: Great leading gets the point across, to be clear.

Activity #1: *The Quiz:* Leaders often have to help teams problem- solve quickly. The challenge of this is that they can overlook details or misunderstand tricky situations. Attention to detail is important.

Activity #2: *Shout It:* Leaders often must translate written info into verbal and then help teams transfer that into action. This is not easy to do, but is a part of organizational achievement.

Peak Performance Assignment: What's one thing you got out of your discussion of the **Lead**Well book?

Notes: One thing I learned from this training meeting:

LeadWell. Ruby Module
Session #7: **Power** (Decisions)

🔑 **Key Concept:** Great leading uses influence well, to help and not hurt people.

L.E.A.D. **Activity #1:** *POWER Up:* We learned the five main sources of power that leaders can tap, to gain influence. Then we practiced identifying examples of these in an exercise.

L.E.A.D. **Activity #2:** *Armed:* We experienced the importance of strategizing power. We also discussed that the one with the most power usually wins, whether or not s/he is right. That's why leaders need to know how to handle power well.

⛰️ **Peak Performance Assignment:** Read Chapter 13 on Power, pages 101-106 in **Lead**Well and respond to the questions.

↩️ **Notes:** One thing I learned from this training session:

LeadWell. Ruby Module
Session #8: Power (Decisions)

Key Concept: Great leading uses influence well, to help and not hurt people.

Peak Performance Assignment: We read Chapter 13 on Power in **Lead**Well and discussed it.   What's one thing you got out of this?

Activity #1: *Power Project:* We experienced a variety of power sources and how they can impact a task, including money, time, talent, and resources. Leaders must help their teams invest these resources wisely.

Notes: One thing I learned from this training session and/or the entire Ruby Module:

LeadYoung. Training Systems © 2013, 2017, 2021 LeadWell Ruby Module
www.LeadYoungTraining.com

Dignity among teammates Respecting those we lead

Power LeadWell

Use influence to help people Know power sources

Communication Make good choices

Make sure the team understands
Do right

Speak effectively Ethics **Honor**

Reflect on what you learned about these 4 leader qualities in this training module. Write some of your ideas here:

The ✸SUCCESS Process*

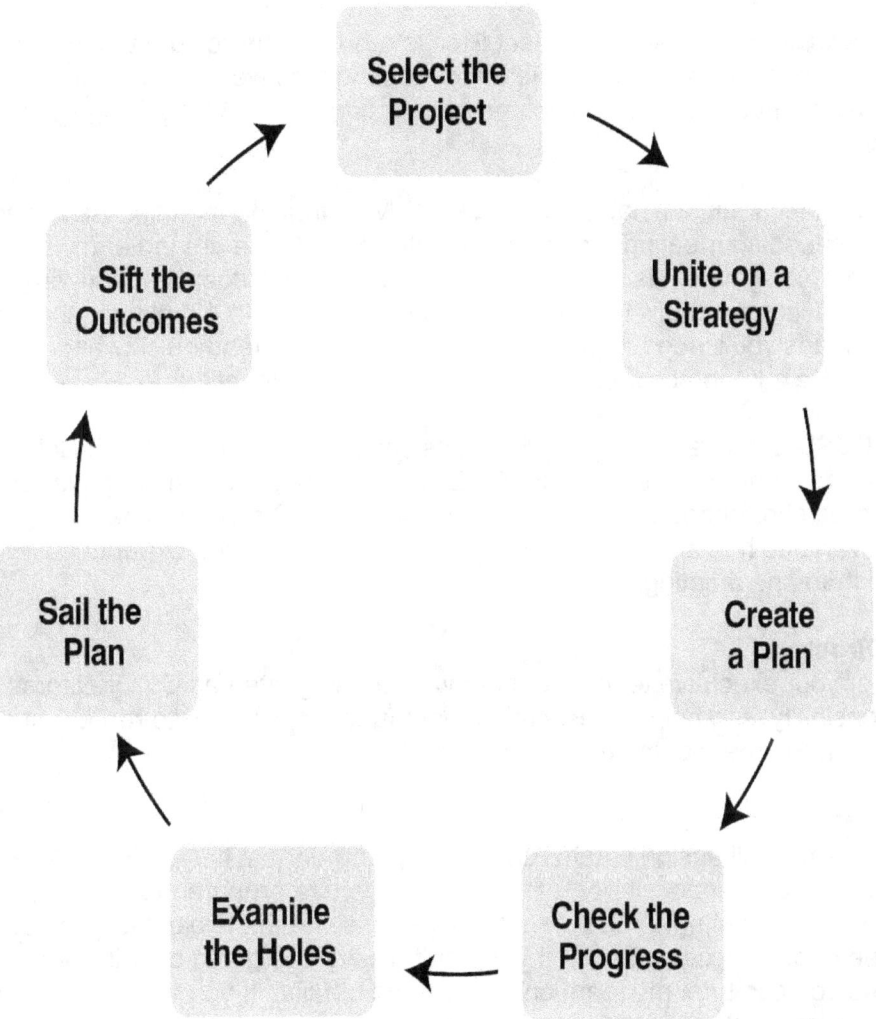

Select the Project

Unite on a Strategy

Create a Plan

Check the Progress

Examine the Holes

Sail the Plan

Sift the Outcomes

* You may need to adjust this process, because leaders do what is necessary to make changes, improve and help the team succeed.

SUCCESS™
Leadership Project Plan

Executive Brief (Overview):

The **SUCCESS** Leadership Project Plan is a guided curriculum that gives young leaders, like you, experience in leading meetings, as well as real world confidence that comes from implementing a project that you'll design and supervise.

This format comprises half of your **Lead**Well. training module. As a leader, you'll be leading meetings much of your life. How these are led and what you achieve through them is vital to the team's and organization's effectiveness. One way we accomplish this is by limiting a single meeting to 12 minutes in length. That means you'll need to prepare ahead of time and lead quickly and efficiently. You'll have a lot to accomplish during each of these meetings.

SUCCESS Leadership Project Plan consists of a 7-step template. Each step makes up an acrostic, spelling SUCCESS. Each of the seven steps is broken into three short meetings. The plan is limited to 6-12 members per project, so that everyone has an opportunity to participate actively and experience leading more than one meeting.

Co-Directors
Two of your executive team members will be designated as Co-Directors. Their responsibility is to help the executive team function well and to represent the team, where needed, in outside settings.

Leader Assignments
Your Trainer will assign you to run meetings throughout this project. When assigned, your responsibility is to make sure you're prepared to run an effective and efficient meeting. You'll want to have reviewed the Project Log to see what has been accomplished, so that you don't waste time going over issues again and so you can brief the team on appropriate details. If you will be gone, be sure your Trainer or Koach knows as far in advance as possible.

Executive Team

Your team represents an executive team. By this we mean that everyone on the team is expected to actually lead others in a task related to this project, in addition to leading meetings.

A typical team would have one or two leaders and several followers. The leader would help the team develop a very detailed plan that it would complete.

But this team is different. We want you to learn leadership. Therefore, you won't be developing all the details needed to accomplish your goal. You'll create a vision, strategy, and plan to the point that everyone knows what it is he or she is responsible to accomplish as a leader. The team can help you if you get stuck, but your primary responsibility is to develop strategic issues and then empower others to handle the tactical details.

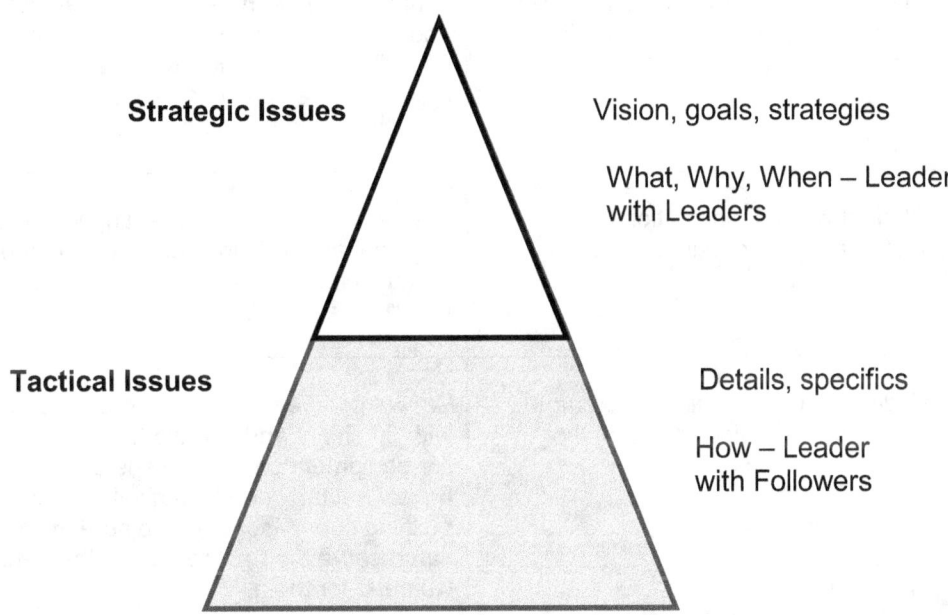

Strategic Issues — Vision, goals, strategies

What, Why, When – Leader with Leaders

Tactical Issues — Details, specifics

How – Leader with Followers

Knowing how much detail to allow will be a challenge. The designated Leader of each meeting, along with your Co-Directors and Trainer and Koach, will need to work together to keep everyone focused on issues that are more strategic than tactical. If tactical details emerge, these can be recorded, but we don't want to invest too much time and energy in our meetings to details. The reason is that details take so much time and this allows each leader to develop a team of people to complete the task. Following are examples of strategic vs. tactical issues, to help you determine where your executive team should be investing its time.

Strategic	Tactical
We need a sign to promote our event, so students can see it	It should be a wooden triangle, covered in cork, but we want to make sure that the flyers are not ripped off by the students like they often do…
We'll line up charities that we'll promote on a monthly basis and provide support for them. Who should contact each one?	The 2nd Harvest people want us to go down to their center and see how we'll bring in some people to put together the food that comes in from donations. Sometimes, they want people who'll just interact with…
We'll create a video that will give a vision of our program, and play it during the school assembly.	Jennie will write the script and then Jess and Sue will do the talking part of the narrative. We'll work with our advisor to make sure he can schedule the video when we need it played.
We'll meet with administration to make sure they approve of our project.	Josh and I will set up a meeting with the Principal and then include a written brief for the school board. I think they meet on the 2nd Tuesday…
We'll do a monthly seminar to promote the community service project of the month.	We want to be sure each room is set up with 30 chairs and that we have the right AV equipment so that the speakers can have what they need. Jeff will contact the building supervisor to make sure that we can reserve the right rooms on the dates we need for them.
We'll do flyers for our promotional support.	We need to make sure they aren't just tossed aside like most of the handouts, so let's be sure that they look good. We can get Amy to do the graphics part and we can see if the school office can run off copies so we can save money. If that doesn't work, we may need to raise some money so we can go get copies made.

Tips for Leading Great Meetings

Just as an athlete works out and practices in order to perform well in a game or event, you're going to be practicing your leading through a series of meetings. Here are some quick tips on running effective meetings. Keep these in mind when it comes your turn to lead as well as analyzing how your fellow leaders are running their meetings.

1. Know Where You've Been: Unless you're the very first meeting leader, you want to provide a brief overview of where you've been, what's been decided, and who's to have done what. That means you'll want to do your homework and know in advance what should be shared, in terms of previous meeting notes and accomplishments. People are busy and can benefit from knowing what has been done so far, so you don't waste time discussing things that have already been discussed. This is especially important when you are the first leader of a meeting after a day or two pause.

2. State the Goal: When you're leading a meeting, your success to a certain degree is based on accomplishing a goal. What is the goal of this meeting and how does it fit in the big picture of your organization? Don't assume that other people know the goal. By declaring the goal and even writing it for people to see, it helps everyone be responsible to stick to the issue. Plus, you can tell if you were effective or not by the end. Obviously, you may need to do some prep work in advance so you know what to say and how you're going to accomplish your goal.

3. Pace Discussion: Ever attend a boring meeting? We all have. Good leaders know how to pace a meeting so that there's enough tension to make it interesting, but not rushed so that people feel that they've not been able to participate. This is a difficult skill to develop, but help talkers get to their point, and know when it's time to change subjects, end a discussion, or engage people who've become bored or started talking to each other instead of the entire group. Pacing is important as a leader.

4. Keep the Focus: Sometimes, meetings can be very interesting, but have little to do with the goal of a meeting. Your job, as meeting leader, is to help your team stay focused on the goal. A good question to ask yourself, when someone is talking is, "What does this have to do with our goal?" If your answer is, "I don't know," then you may want to ask the speaker, "Justin, help me understand what this has to do with the goal of our meeting."

5. Manage Personalities: Every team has different temperaments, with various experiences, intelligence, and emotions. What you want to do as a leader is help everyone work together to accomplish the goal of the meeting. This may require you to calm a conflict, to help people who feel confident in talking to do some listening, and encourage more quiet people to express their ideas. Doing this in a caring, honoring way is difficult. Try to stay positive. Smile. Make eye contact. And use the names of people to make them feel honored.

6. Seek Broad but Not Necessarily Even Input: Everyone doesn't need to share equally, but everyone should share. You want to make sure that individuals do not dominate the meeting while a few remain silent. There are nice ways of asking people who've talked a lot to listen, and encouraging ways for quiet people to share their ideas. "John, what do you think about this?" "Let's have some of you who've not shared yet, tell us what you're thinking."

7. Consider Mini-Meetings & Sub-Teams: One way to gain a lot of ideas quickly, and help people feel like they've participated, is to break up into groups of 2-4, and then assign them 1-3 minutes for brainstorming, discussion, or strategizing. By doing this, you can maximize the time spent when just one person would have been talking. Plus, quieter people feel more comfortable sharing their thoughts with 1-3 others, instead of groups of 6-12. You can assign different tasks for each sub-team, or let them all work on the same issue. Then let each team report on what they discussed.

8. Stand or Sit? Sometimes it's good to stand when you're leading a meeting, and sometimes it's better to sit. Sitting creates more of a feel that we're all on the same level. And if there are 8 or fewer people in a small room, standing may seem awkward, as people look at your stomach instead of your face. Standing is good if the room is large, you're writing on a whiteboard or flip chart, and if you need a bit more authority for whatever reason. It says, "I'm in charge" more than if you're sitting.

9. Write or Not Write? When you're the meeting leader, sometimes you'll want to write ideas on a flip chart or whiteboard. The benefit is that your team can see what is being discussed and your scribe can record what is posted. The question is whether or not you should do it yourself, or select someone else. If it is a potentially controversial subject, you may want to do the writing yourself so you can select the words you prefer, reduce wording that is emotion-laden, and even put the words in a way that you want as a leader, thus creating more control. The benefit of asking someone else to write, instead of you, is that you can keep your eyes on the team and you don't turn your back on them while they wait for you to write. If your writing isn't clear, find someone who writes well.

10. Review & Record: Before the meeting ends, you'll want to be sure that your scribe has a sense of what should be recorded. You can provide your own overview of what was accomplished, or you may want to ask your scribe to do that. Be sure you end your regular meeting in time for you to provide a 1-2 minute overview of what was accomplished, and if possible, talk about HOW the team functioned. Then thank them.

The next page provides a summary of ideas you'll want to keep in mind as you prepare to lead your meetings.

Prep	• Make sure you know what the theme of the meeting is, along with the goal. • Is there anything you need to update your team on, such as a reminder of previous decisions in meetings and anything the Trainer or Co-Directors did that might affect this meeting?
Start	• Stand or sit in a place where you can clearly see team members. • Speak up; make eye contact. • Read/state the meeting goal. • Name your Scribe, Time Keeper, and if like, a person to write on the whiteboard/flip chart as you speak.
Meeting	• Get team members to participate, but be aware of those talking too much and not enough. • As you lead, be aware of what's happening among the team members. • Keep the conversations on track, summarizing what's been said and including your opinions. • Ask for a vote if needed, or whatever next steps are needed. • Be aware of the practices for running effective meetings as well as the common challenges (next page), so you can **Lead**Well.
Wrap-up	• Allow for 1-2 minutes at the end to summarize what has been discussed and especially what has been decided. • State that the meeting is adjourned and thank everyone for participating. • Listen to GBB feedback and thank the responders for sharing their thoughts.
Follow-up	• Co-Directors need to work with the Trainer to be sure any unfinished business is taken care of so the project stays on track. • Co-Directors should follow-up on Leaders who've been assigned tasks, to make sure they follow through. • Leaders (team members) should follow up on responsibilities created in the meetings.

10 Common Meeting Leading Mistakes

1. **Not sticking to the point of the meeting.** As the meeting leader, it is your responsibility to keep your team focused on achieving the stated goal. This is not an easy task, but it is your main job.

2. **Not providing sufficient review on what's been covered.** If you don't clarify where you've been and what you've done, you'll often waste time going over things you've already achieved.

3. **Wasting time.** There's a place for fun, humor, and stories, but usually it's not in these short meetings, where you have a limited amount of time to get a lot accomplished. Begin promptly and end on time!

4. **Letting someone in the group dominate the discussion.** Be sure everyone gets to participate. Don't jump on an idea just because a strong person raises it. Be kind but direct in hearing from others.

5. **Getting sidetracked.** Sometimes, you need to discuss an issue that is raised, but don't let that keep you from your task. Keep your team on purpose.

6. **Failure to listen well.** Leading a meeting doesn't mean doing all the talking. You want to model good listening to team members as you help them stay on the point.

7. **Failure to speak up and share your thoughts.** Your team is looking for you to cast your opinion and help them develop consensus, so be sure to leave your influence on the meeting.

8. **Getting caught up in details instead of strategic thinking.** Remember, this is an executive team, meaning you are delegating the details to them to take care of in their own meetings.

9. **Failing to establish clear action steps and assure good note taking.** Who is going to do what, and when? Be sure the scribe has a clear sense of what was decided in order to write good notes.

10. **Not summarizing the meeting.** What did you accomplish? Leave time at the end to provide a good summary before you end.

LeadYoung Training Systems © 2013, 2017, 2021 LeadWell Ruby Module
www.LeadYoungTraining.com

SUCCESS™

Leadership Project Plan
Meeting Assignments

Here are the tentative meeting assignments. Look for your name and then review the meeting description so you can be prepared ahead of time. If you realize that you won't be available, talk to your Trainer right away. The (#) denotes the page number where instructions are found in the Leader Manual. (If you have more than 1 team, note this team's members at the end of the next page.)

Co-Director _____

Co-Director _____

Select the Project

Meeting #1 Determine the Project (35-36): _____

Meeting #2 Create a Vision Statement (37): _____

Meeting #3 Establish Goal Measurements (38): _____

Unite on a Strategy

Meeting #1: Define Tasks & Resources (40): _____

Meeting #2: Strategic Brainstorm (41-42): _____

Meeting #3: Select Best Ideas (43): _____

Create a Plan

Meeting #1: Design a Plan (45): _____

Meeting #2: Chart Your Plan (46): _____

Meeting #3: Assign Responsibilities (47): _____

LeadYoung Training Systems © 2013, 2017, 2021 LeadWell Ruby Module
www.LeadYoungTraining.com

Check the Progress

Meeting #1: Check In (49): _____

Meeting # 2: Report & Refine (50): _____

Meeting # 3: Review & Confirm (51): _____

Examine the Holes

Meeting #1: Check In & Troubleshoot (53): _____

Meeting #2: Troubleshoot/Pre-Mortem (54): _____

Meeting #3: Finalize Our Jobs (55): _____

Sail the Plan (*tentative meeting assignments follow*)

Meeting #1: Pre-Huddle (57-59): _____

Meeting #2: Event/Launch (57-59): _____

Meeting #3: Post-Huddle (57-59): _____

Sift the Outcomes

Meeting #1: Post-Mortem (60): _____

Meeting #2: Gleanings (61): _____

Meeting #3: Celebration (62): _____

(Be sure to note any changes/updates)

LeadYoung Training Systems © 2013, 2017, 2021 LeadWell Ruby Module
www.LeadYoungTraining.com

✴ SUCCESS™: *A 7-Step Project Development Outline for Youth Leadership Training*

Introduction:
- Establish the importance of this learning process.
- Introduce S.U.C.C.E.S.S. steps & sub-meetings.
- Announce Co-Directors of the Executive Team.
- Announce meeting assignments.
- Explain giving & receiving GBB Feedback.
- Receive 2-4 project ideas to be discussed in the next meeting.

Select the project: We'll determine WHAT we're going to do and perhaps WHY. Then we'll set a measurable goal and write a vision statement for clarity and inspiration.*

Unite on a strategy: We'll identify a variety of ways of HOW we might accomplish our goal. Then we'll determine what ideas are the best, while not focusing on details yet.**

Create a plan: We'll create a plan as to how we'll accomplish our goal. Then we'll create a graphic of the plan and assign responsibilities and expectations. ***

Check the progress: Team leaders will report on their progress. We'll re-evaluate the plan, make adjustments, and troubleshoot any problems that have arisen.

Examine the holes: We'll investigate blind spots and troubleshoot as needed. If all is good, we'll do a "pre-mortem." Then we'll synchronize final details before we "Sail the Plan."

Sail the plan: Depending on the project, we'll run the event or launch the program. This will require a variety of real-time, on-the-job leadership actions. Our Directors will oversee our executive team.

Sift the outcomes: We'll review how the project went and what we learned about leading. This will include a post-mortem, how we might do things differently next time, and a celebration with our executive team.

LeadYoung Training Systems © 2013, 2017, 2021 LeadWell Ruby Module
www.LeadYoungTraining.com

Because **SUCCESS** is a modestly flexible template, additional meetings may be needed at key times, such as the following:

Optional Addendum: Idea Brainstorm: You may want to divide the project selection into 2 parts. Part 1 would be an open brainstorm session to come up with plausible ideas. Part 2 would be the selection of the project after settling of thought and some research was completed.

**Optional Addendum: Gain the Support: In real world situations, projects often require sponsorship from other agencies. This may include transportation, a legal entity, or the overall organization. A presentation to sponsors may be required to obtain permission.

*** Optional Addendum: Assess the talent: When considering a project, talent, skill, and experience are important. In this optional step, you can determine what tasks are involved in your project and who might best oversee specific tasks and sub-teams. This may also take place after the "create a plan" step.

Although structured, the goal of this outline is to provide sufficient detail to cover the basics of most projects, but also allow sufficient flexibility to fit changes in plans and challenges that arise. After all, that's what leaders do. Note that each phrase in the acrostic begins with a verb, denoting action.

Plus, we want to emphasize the four concepts that are being taught in the first part of the curriculum. This provides an opportunity to create an awareness of how these look in the context of a real project. We'll provide ideas in the script, but feel free to continually bring them up to reinforce the learning.

During each meeting, there are five roles:
- Meeting Leader (selected in advance by the Trainer)
- Scribe (person who writes meetings notes in the journal, selected by the Leader)
- Time Keeper (person who keeps track of the time and announces "5 minutes," "2 minutes," and "Time's Up").
- Responders #1 & #2 (people who write a GBB card and give a 30-second report at the end of the meeting, selected by the Trainer).

The Meeting Leader may also want to delegate the task of writing on the whiteboard / flip chart, if desired.

Select the Project

The focus here is WHAT & WHY, not HOW. What do we want to accomplish, how are we going to measure our success, and what are the basic tasks and resources needed?

Key points:
- Announce that the goal of this session is to select a leadership project that we'll take turns planning, and then act on the plan.
- IF we come up with ideas on HOW we're going to accomplish this, we'll write them down so we can use them later.
- We'll be conducting three short meetings. The Meeting Leader's responsibility is to keep us on track, monitoring the time and group dynamics.
- The Meeting Leader will select a Scribe who'll take notes in the Project Journal and a Time Keeper to remind us of 5 and 2 minutes left, and then stop us at 13 minutes total.
- The Trainer will select two responders who'll each provide a 30- second Good-Better-Best feedback and a written card for the Leader.
- At the end, provide a summary of the meeting results in order to help transition to the next meeting and/or session.

Meeting #1: Determine the Project: Your responsibility is to lead your team in determining <u>what</u> it will accomplish among the ideas provided. You'll want to explain the project in a 10-30 word description. You only have 12 minutes to accomplish this.

1-Minute Review: Good, Better, Best

Meeting #2: Create a Vision Statement: Your responsibility is to lead your team in establishing an "elevator speech" that is clear, inspirational, and brief. You'll want to record this in such a way that your entire team can communicate it effectively (20-50 words). You only have 12 minutes to accomplish this.

1-Minute Review: Good, Better, Best

Meeting #3: Establish Goal Measurements: Your responsibility is to lead your team in creating specific ways to measure your goal, so you'll know how successful you are and to help you design a practical plan. You only have 12 minutes to accomplish this.

1-Minute Review: Good, Better, Best

Session #1: Select the Project   Meeting #1: Determine the Project

Leader Meeting Instructions: Your responsibility is to lead your team in determining <u>what</u> it will accomplish among the ideas provided. You'll want to explain the project in a 10-30 written word description. You only have 12 minutes to accomplish this. Assign the Time Keeper and Scribe for this meeting. The Trainer will select two Responders for feedback.

Leader, read this aloud: *This meeting is to determine what it is we want to accomplish for a team project. We've reviewed some suggestions, so now we want to determine what we believe is important and achievable by our team. We don't need to establish the size of the goal. We'll do that in the next meeting. We have 12 minutes to determine our project from the ideas presented and then describe it in 10-30 written words.*

Ideas:

- Get people's opinions on the ideas your Trainer presented. What seems most feasible? Use the three qualifiers on the following page.

- You may want to list the pros and cons (positives and negatives) of each item on a flip chart or whiteboard.

- Three voting options:
    - Post the ideas on a wall. Give everyone two sticky notes. Ask everyone to vote by placing one or two sticky notes on their favorite.
    - Ask people to vote for only one, by having them raise their hands as you announce each one.
    - Ask everyone to provide a "consensus." This is not an exact vote as it is a sense of general agreement.

- After a vote has been taken and you select the final project, ask if there are any more comments. You want to provide opportunities for people to share their concerns that up to now they may not have shared.

- State the project, and then thank everyone for their participation. Receive 1-minute feedback on your portion of meeting leading, and thank the Responders for the feedback.

✔ Leadership Project Plan

- ## Sizable: What constitutes a good, potential project idea? Apply the "Goldilocks test." (Remember the fable of Goldilocks and the three bears?) You don't want a project too small or too large, but rather just right. In order to do that, you'll need to know your students (how available, confident, and resourced they are), and also the project dynamics (i.e. host charity, access to gatekeepers, organizational schedule, policy and legal procedures). The size of the project needs to be realistic for a team of teens to accomplish with a moderate degree of success. Attempting to raise $1,000,000 may be inspiring, but is more apt to produce frustration, overshadowing teachable steps toward leading big.

- ## Soon: This specific project needs to have a short start and end time, preferably within one month of finishing the final planning meeting. For example, a year-long program for after-school reading is not apt to be measurable for feedback. Try to focus on a single event, even if it is the launch phase of a larger, ongoing project. If you're doing this as part of a summer camp setting, you'll want to accomplish the project on Thursday or Friday, followed by the debrief and celebration.

- ## Leadership Oriented: This needs to be run by teens (vs. merely staffed). For example, using teens to staff someone else's event isn't about leading. Plus, there need to be enough aspects of this project that would truly allow everyone an opportunity to lead one facet of the project. For example, everyone should be in charge of leading or co-leading part of the project that involves other people, not just something they can do alone. That means you'll have multiple sub-teams that will coordinate together for the final goal.

Hopefully, your Trainer and/or Co-Directors have done some prep work so you'll be provided 2-4 project ideas from which to choose. Either way, use these three filters to select your Leadership Project.

 **Lead**Well

Session #1: Select the Project   Meeting #2: Create a Vision Statement

Leader Meeting Instructions: Your responsibility is to lead your team in establishing an "elevator speech" that is clear, inspirational, and brief. You'll want to record this in such a way that your entire team can communicate it effectively. You only have 12 minutes to accomplish this.
Assign the Time Keeper and Scribe for this meeting. The Trainer will select two Responders for feedback.

Leader, read this aloud: *This meeting is to create a clear, verbal vision statement for this project, so that all of us can communicate the same thing to others. A vision connects with a person's mind and heart. Let's say we have 30 seconds in an elevator with a new person or an important leader. What would we say to communicate this vision? We'll have 12 minutes to write a clear, inspirational description.*

Ideas:

- Restate the project that the team just agreed to pursue.

- Ask team members for their ideas on what seems feasible in terms of size (e.g. number attending event, amount of money raised) and reasonable time (e.g. by the end of the semester, on December 2).
  - Discuss pros and cons of these ideas
  - Look for a challenging but reasonable goal

- Write a simple "elevator speech" that quickly tells a stranger what your project goal is. There should also be an inspirational factor to it, something that will tug at people's hearts and emotions.

- Write a 20-50 word vision statement. If you don't get this done, then delegate someone to present it at the next session.

- If ideas are shared on HOW you might accomplish this, you can write them down, but these will be for a later meeting.

- Remember to thank everyone for their participation and announce that this portion of the meeting is now adjourned. Receive 1- minute feedback on your portion of meeting leading, and thank your Responders for the feedback.

LeadYoung. Training Systems © 2013, 2017, 2021 LeadWell Ruby Module
www.LeadYoungTraining.com

Session #1: Select the Project   Meeting #3: Establish Goal Measurements

Leader Meeting Instructions: Your responsibility is to lead your team in creating specific ways to measure your goal, so you'll know how successful you are and to help you design a practical plan. You only have 12 minutes to accomplish this. Assign the Time Keeper and Scribe for this meeting. The Trainer will select two Responders for feedback.

Leader, read this aloud: *This meeting is to determine establishing measurable goals to help us know if we're successful or not. A quantitative goal measures an amount, such as how many people attend an event or how much money is raised. A quality goal measures how much people learn, or how much they like something at the end compared to at the start. We can use things such as counts, surveys, and interviews to measure our goal. We have 12 minutes to decide on 2-3 ways we plan to measure our goal.*

Ideas:
- Restate the project and the goals that you've just established in this meeting.

- Come up with 2-3 clear, written ways to measure your goal:
  - Quantity: For example, How many will attend? How much money will be raised?
  - Quality: For example, We'll survey people before and after the event and we'll see an improvement in their attitude/knowledge. People will complete a survey and we'll average 4.0 or better on a 5-point scale.

- Remember to thank everyone for their participation and announce that this portion of the meeting is now adjourned. Receive 1- minute feedback on your portion of meeting leading, and thank the Responders for the feedback.

The Trainer should summarize what happened in Session #1 and comment on how the four module concepts were involved. Then s/he will introduce what will take place in the next portion of this process, and announce the next Leaders.

Unite on a Strategy

The big picture is determining a variety of ways of HOW we can accomplish our goal. Then we'll determine what ideas are the best along with a draft of a plan goal and a basic strategy on how to accomplish it, including timelines, milestones, and primary tasks. There are probably several ways to accomplish our goal, but we'll want to strategize on the best for our team. This is NOT a detailed plan, but a basic strategy for major tasks.

Key points:
- Restate what your project goal is from the journal notes of the previous SUCCESS session.
- Announce that the goal of this session is to brainstorm and determine the best strategy to accomplish our goal.
- We'll be conducting three short meetings. The leader's responsibility is to keep us on track, monitoring the time and group dynamics.
- Assign a Time Keeper and a Scribe to take notes in the journal.
- At the end, provide a summary of the meeting results in order to help transition to the next meeting and/or session.

Meeting #1: Define Tasks & Resources: Your responsibility is to break the goal into tasks and resources required to accomplish the goal. For example, a typical project may have tasks such as marketing/promotion, recruiting people, and talking to administration, and require resources such as a room, copies, sound system, etc. We'll have 12 minutes to make a list of the tasks and resources it will take to accomplish our goal.

1-Minute Review: Good, Better, Best

Meeting #2: Strategic Brainstorm: Your responsibility is to lead the team in brainstorming possible strategies for accomplishing the goal and the tasks. At this point, you want quantity more than quality, so you'll want to come up with as many ideas as possible. You have 12 minutes to do this.

1-Minute Review: Good, Better, Best

Meeting #3: Select Best Ideas: Your responsibility is to lead the team in creating the start of a written plan that identifies tasks and resources, along with how they work together to accomplish our goals. You have 12 minutes to do this.

1-Minute Review: Good, Better, Best

Session #2: Unite on a Strategy   Meeting #1: Define Tasks & Resources

Leader Meeting Instructions: Your responsibility is to break the goal into tasks and resources required to accomplish the goal. For example, a typical project may have tasks such as marketing/promotion, recruiting people, and talking to administration, and require resources such as a room, copies, sound system, etc. We'll have 12 minutes to make a list of the tasks and resources it will take to accomplish our goal.

Leader, read this aloud: *This meeting is to determine the various tasks and resources it will take to accomplish our goal. We want to figure out what we may have or not have. We'll create a list of these categories and tasks and resources so we can then brainstorm ways of using and obtaining them.*

Ideas:

- Restate the project and the goals that you've just established in this meeting. PLUS, ask the Scribe to read the Vision Statement that was to be finished from the previous session.

- Ask the team members for their ideas on what resources and actions will be needed to accomplish the goal in the stated time.
    - This is NOT about assigning tasks yet. It's simply developing a list of "things to do" and resources to get. You can write HOW items for later use.
    - Don't waste time on tiny details.

- You may want to discuss categories of items, such as marketing, resources needed, recruiting talent/people, obtaining a location, and budget.

- You can decide to write these ideas and organize them on a flip chart or whiteboard or ask someone else to do this, allowing you to interact better. You'll want to leave these up for following meetings.

- Remember to thank everyone for their participation and announce that this portion of the meeting is now adjourned. Receive 1- minute feedback on your portion of meeting leading, and thank your Responders for the feedback.

Session #2: Unite on a Strategy   Meeting #2: Strategic Brainstorm

Leader Meeting Instructions: Read the "Brainstorming Guidelines." Then begin brainstorming solutions, based on the tasks and resources you came up with in the last meeting. Try to avoid getting too detailed on any single topic. Then review your progress. You only have 12 minutes to accomplish this. Assign the Time Keeper and Scribe for this meeting. The Trainer will select two Responders for feedback.

Leader, read this aloud: *This meeting is to introduce guidelines for a good brainstorm session* (see the following page) *and then make a list of ideas of how to accomplish our goal, based on the tasks and resources we just listed. We have 12 minutes to accomplish this goal, but we'll have more time in the next meeting, too.*

Ideas:
- Restate the project and the goals that you've just established in this meeting.

- Establish categories for brainstorming if you think that would be helpful. Put these on the whiteboard/flip chart, select a category, and start the brainstorming. Another way of doing this is the inverse, where you write the ideas and then try to put them into categories of topic. You choose what to do. As much as possible, build on what you've previously discussed in other meetings.

- Consider these options:
  - Let everyone brainstorm as a large team, but have them raise their hands so only one is talking at a time.
  - Give everyone sticky notes to write one idea per note and then put them on the wall. Then sort them by categories.
  - Divide the team into 2s, 3s, or 4s to come up with ideas and then share them with everyone.

- Remember to thank everyone for their participation and announce that this portion of the meeting is now adjourned. Receive 1- minute feedback on your portion of meeting leading, and thank your Responders for the feedback.

**LeadWell**

Session #2: Unite on a Strategy   Meeting #2: Strategic Brainstorm

Effective Brainstorming Guidelines

Meeting Leader, Please Read Aloud:

The primary purpose of a good brainstorm session is to tap the creativity of team members in certain areas. The main goal is not the quality of the ideas, but the quantity. How many can we come up with in a short period of time?

For this to happen, there are two basic guidelines that people use.

#1. There are no bad ideas. Obviously, some may seem better than others, but if someone says, "That's stupid," or "No, that won't work," people stop sharing because they don't want to be judged. The best design companies have learned that some of their best ideas come after a few crazy ones are mentioned.

#2. Remember, quantity more than quality. We may want to set a goal for a certain number and write them down so we can see them. This helps us avoid repeating what we've already said and helps the Scribe write things down in case we need them later.

Finally, we'll come up with a separate list for each of the main tasks we came up with in the last Session. In our 3rd meeting in this Session, we'll select what we think are the best ideas for this project, so feel free to be creative during this meeting and the next.

If anyone goes against these rules, the Meeting Leader is responsible for reminding everyone to stick to the guidelines and stay on topic.

Session #2: Unite on a Strategy   Meeting #3: Select Best Ideas

Leader Meeting Instructions: Your responsibility is to lead the group in determining what ideas are the best ones, so that your team can prioritize them. Record the final ideas in preparation for the next Session meetings. You only have 12 minutes to accomplish this. Assign the Time Keeper and Scribe for this meeting. The Trainer will select two Responders for feedback.

Leader, read this aloud: *This meeting is to determine a list of the best ideas of how to accomplish our goal, using the list of ideas that we brainstormed. We have 12 minutes to accomplish this goal.*

Ideas:
- Restate the project and the goals that you've just established in this meeting.

- Take one category at a time, if you have categories, and determine the best ideas based on what is achievable.

- Have people discuss the pros and cons of the ideas. This can take a lot of time, so try to keep them focused on the task and aware of the time.

- Another option is to have three categories: Best Ideas, Those Unrealistic, and If We're Able. Be sure the Scribe has the best ideas recorded.

- Remember to thank everyone for their participation and announce that this portion of the meeting is now adjourned. Receive 1- minute feedback on your portion of meeting leading, and thank your Responders for the feedback.

The Trainer should summarize what happened in Session #2 and comment on how the four module concepts were involved. Then s/he will introduce what will take place in the next portion of this process, and announce the next Leaders.

Create a Plan

Establish a plan as to how you can accomplish the goal. Consider available resources, and assign key roles to people for further development and preparation.

Key points:
- Restate what your project goal is from the journal notes of the first SUCCESS session. Restate your strategy from the notes on the previous session.
- Announce that the goal of this session is to develop a plan of what we're going to do, and then assign tasks to people on the team.
- We want to come up with assignments that are NOT too detailed, because we want the leaders to figure out how to accomplish them on their own.
- We want the tasks clear enough to hand them off to each leader so that s/he understands what is expected.
- We'll be conducting three short meetings. The leader's responsibility is to keep us on track, monitoring the time and group dynamics.
- At the end, provide a summary of the meeting results in order to help transition to the next meeting and/or session.

Meeting #1: Design a Plan: Your responsibility is to create a basic plan for the project that includes the tasks, resources, and brainstorm ideas that you developed. You have 12 minutes to do this.

1-Minute Review: Good, Better, Best

Meeting #2: Chart Your Plan: Your goal in this meeting is to create a visual aid that depicts your plan, so all can see how it will work. Then a master chart will be developed and posted. You have 12 minutes to do this.

1-Minute Review: Good, Better, Best

Meeting #3: Assign Responsibilities: Your responsibility is to lead the meeting in determining who on the executive team is going to lead what. The goal is for each person to lead or co-lead a task team, not just do things on their own. You have 12 minutes to do this.

1-Minute Review: Good, Better, Best

Session #3: Create a Plan   Meeting #1: Design a Plan

Leader Meeting Instructions: Create a basic plan for the project that includes the tasks, resources, and brainstorm ideas that you developed. You only have 12 minutes to accomplish this. Assign the Time Keeper and Scribe for this meeting. The Trainer will select two Responders for feedback.

Leader, read this aloud: *This meeting is to determine the primary tasks required to accomplish the large goal and place them in sequence to begin a timeline. We're going to list the things necessary so that we can later assign responsibilities to some of you. We don't need to come up with a detailed plan now. We'll do more of that in the next meeting. Let's think of the major tasks and what each will take in terms of money, time, talent, and resources. We have 12minutes to determine a goal from the ideas presented.*

Ideas:
- Restate the project and the goals that you established in the last meeting.

- On a flip chart or whiteboard, begin listing the tasks required to accomplish the goal. You can do this a few ways, but pick one that makes sense to you:
  - Think in terms of sequence or progress. Starting from the beginning, walk everyone through the process and determine the tasks.
  - Consider larger categories, such as publicity/advertising, gathering equipment, organizing the team, clean-up, follow-up (or whatever fits your situation).

- Include items in the tasks such as time, money, talent, and so on.

- Review your accomplishments by stating the main tasks.

- Remember to thank everyone for their participation and announce that this portion of the meeting is now adjourned.

- Receive 1-minute feedback on your portion of meeting leading, and thank your Responders for the feedback.

LeadWell

Session #3: Create a Plan   Meeting #2: Chart Your Plan

Leader Meeting Instructions: Your responsibility is to divide your group into 2-3 teams to create a visual aid that depicts our plan. Then you'll have each team share theirs and have everyone say the parts they like best, so you can create a single chart to post. You only have 12 minutes to accomplish this. Assign the Time Keeper and Scribe for this meeting. The Trainer will select two Responders for feedback.

Leader, read this aloud: *This meeting is to create a visual aid that describes our plan. Everyone will have a sheet of poster board or flip chart paper and 8 minutes to draw shapes and lines and then label them, so we can see a visual presentation. Then we'll put them on the wall, describe them, and say what we liked about each. Then we'll assign 2-3 people to create a final chart that we'll keep on the wall. We have 12 minutes to determine a goal from the ideas presented.*

Ideas:
- Restate the project and the goals of your leadership project.

- Make sure you have adequate resources (including fresh markers) ready for the teams (and tape and push pins to hang the charts).

- As the meeting Leader, your role is to walk around and help the teams stay on task and keep track of the pace.

- Then facilitate the discussion of each and the accumulation of the best ideas, as well as who should create a final chart that will be posted so everyone can see.

- Remember to thank everyone for their participation and announce that this portion of the meeting is now adjourned.

- Receive 1-minute feedback on your portion of meeting leading, and thank your Responders for the feedback.

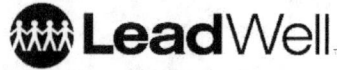

Session #3: Create a Plan   Meeting #3: Assign Responsibilities

Leader Meeting Instructions: Your responsibility is to lead the meeting in determining who on the executive team is going to lead what. The goal is for each person to lead or co-lead a task team, not just do things on their own. You only have 12 minutes to accomplish this. Assign the Time Keeper and Scribe for this meeting. The Trainer will select two Responders .

Leader, read this aloud: *This meeting is to assign responsibilities to your executive team. We want to make sure that everyone has an opportunity to lead, and not just follow, so we may co-lead parts of the plan. We have 12 minutes to determine a goal from the ideas presented.*

Ideas:
- Discuss talents and resources needed for the various tasks:
  - You may or may not want to ask for volunteers. Be sure everyone has a task. Consider assigning co-leaders to be sure that everyone has a chance to lead and to help any team members who are not as strong at leading.
  - Availability: If a certain task takes a lot of time, or must be done in a week, you'll need to determine that.
  - Network: If you need to recruit talent outside of the team, someone with contacts in that area should be in charge.

- Determine the best fit for each of the tasks and make assignments to people. Be sure everyone on the team has a role, and as much as possible, try to make it a leadership role, not just serving. See how you can get the members to create their own team or take turns leading fellow team members toward the task, versus doing the task alone. (The Co-Directors won't get a task as they coordinate everyone.)

- Thank the team for their participation, and receive 1-minute feedback on your portion of meeting leading. Thank your Responders for the feedback.

The Trainer should summarize what happened in Session #3 and comment on how the four module concepts were involved. Then s/he will introduce what will take place in the next portion of this process, and announce the next Leaders.

Check the Progress

Ask appropriate team leaders to check in, provide updates on preliminary process, and advise on next steps that can be implemented. Clarify expectations.

Key points:
- Restate what your project goal is from the log notes of the first SUCCESS session. Review key points from the previous session.
- Announce that the goal of this session is to ask team members to provide updates on their areas of responsibility and clarify next steps.
- We'll be conducting three short meetings. The leader's responsibility is to keep us on track, monitoring the time and group dynamics.
- Assign a Time Keeper and a Scribe to take notes in the meeting log.
- Generally, the "Gel" method is recommended in this situation versus "Tell," "Sell," or "Del" style of leading.
- At the end, provide a summary of the meeting results in order to help transition to the next meeting and/or session.

Meeting #1: Check In: Your responsibility is to lead the team members in reporting on their plans. You'll identify (but not solve) people or tasks that may seem to need further development that will be addressed in the next meeting. You have 12 minutes to accomplish this.

1-Minute Review: Good, Better, Best

Meeting #2: Report & Refine: Your responsibility is to lead the team in further discussion and brainstorming of solutions and plans that are not progressing at this point. You may need to assist in refining the plans. You have 12 minutes to accomplish this.

1-Minute Review: Good, Better, Best

Meeting #3: Review & Confirm: Your responsibility is to go over the goal, strategy, and tasks you've planned so far and see what you might be missing or what else needs to be discussed at this time. You have 12 minutes to accomplish this.

1-Minute Review: Good, Better, Best

Session #4: Check the Progress   Meeting #1: Check In

Leader Meeting Instructions: Your responsibility is to lead the team members in reporting on their plans. You'll identify (but not solve) people or tasks that may seem to need further development that will be addressed in the next meeting. You only have 12 minutes to accomplish this. Assign the Time Keeper and Scribe for this meeting. The Trainer will select two Responders for feedback.

Leader, read aloud: *This meeting is designed for us to check in and report on what we've done in our specific areas of assignment from our last meeting. We won't spend a lot of time on any one issue, but will come back to issues in the next meeting if we need to work on them. We have 12 minutes to do this.*

Ideas:
- Restate the project and the goals of your leadership project.

- Based on your notes (or a flip chart or whiteboard you've prepared), ask each leader to give a verbal update on what he or she has been doing.

- Note areas where you may need to spend more time fixing problems or brainstorming solutions in the next meeting. Write these on a flip chart/whiteboard so the next leader can come back to them.

- Review your accomplishments by going over who reported in and what items you'll want to discuss further in the next meeting.

- Remember to thank everyone for their participation and announce that this portion of the meeting is now adjourned.

- Receive 1- minute feedback on your portion of meeting leading, and thank your Responders for the feedback.

Session #4: Check the Progress   Meeting #2: Report & Refine

Leader Meeting Instructions: Your responsibility is to lead the team in further discussion and brainstorming of solutions and plans that are not progressing at this point. You may need to assist in refining the plans. You only have 12 minutes to accomplish this. Assign the Time Keeper and Scribe for this meeting. The Trainer will select two Responders for feedback.

Leader, read aloud: *This meeting is to provide further support and planning for specific tasks that may have had problems or that need to be changed. We have 12 minutes to determine a goal from the ideas presented.*

Ideas:

- Restate the leadership project and the goal.

- Refer to the items on the flip chart/whiteboard. Determine which seems to be the priority and do that first.

- Keep an eye on the time, but do what is necessary to help the team in resolving the issues.

- Review your accomplishments.

- Remember to thank everyone for their participation and announce that this portion of the meeting is now adjourned.

- Receive 1-minute feedback on your portion of meeting leading, and thank your Responders for the feedback.

Session #4: Check the Progress   Meeting #3: Review & Confirm

Leader Meeting Instructions: Your responsibility is to go over the goal, strategy, and tasks you've planned so far, and see what you might be missing or what else needs to be discussed at this time. You only have 12 minutes to accomplish this. Assign the Time Keeper and Scribe for this meeting. The Trainer will select two Responders for feedback.

Leader, read aloud: *This meeting is to go over the plan once again to be sure we've covered what is necessary. We can continue to work on items that were not resolved in the previous meeting. We have 12 minutes to determine a goal from the ideas presented.*

Ideas:

- Restate the project and the goals of your leadership project.

- Refer to the flip chart/whiteboard items and see what else needs to be accomplished in this meeting.

- Step back and see if you missed something in the plan. Go over it again and see if people have additional ideas or concerns.

- Ask the Time Keeper to give you 5-, 2-, and 1-minute reminders so you can pace your meeting.

- Review your accomplishments by stating the plan. Announce the date/time of the next meeting.

- Remember to thank everyone for their participation and announce that this portion of the meeting is now adjourned.

- Receive 1-minute feedback on your portion of meeting leading and thank your team for the feedback.

The Trainer should summarize what happened in Session #4 and comment on how the four module concepts were involved. Then s/he will introduce what will take place in the next portion of this process, and announce the next Leaders.

Examine the Holes

Investigate early steps and confirm that the strategies and plans are workable. Troubleshoot initial challenges. What are possible blind spots and how large are they? What could go wrong at this point?

Key points:
- Restate what your project goal is from the log notes of the first SUCCESS session. Review what you accomplished in the previous session and what needed to be prepared for this session.
- Announce that the goal of this session is to analyze current and potential problems, and brainstorm solutions to reduce risks of failure and increase the chances for success.
- We'll be conducting three short meetings. The leader's responsibility is to keep us on track, monitoring the time and group dynamics.
- Assign a Time Keeper and a Scribe to take notes in the meeting log.
- Generally, the "Gel" method is recommended in this situation versus "Tell," "Sell," or "Del" style of leading.
- At the end, provide a summary of the meeting results in order to help transition to the next meeting and/or session.

Meeting #1: Check In & Troubleshoot: Your responsibility is to lead your team in hearing progress reports on what has been done, including a discussion of facing challenges by noting them on a flip chart or whiteboard. You have 12 minutes to accomplish this.

1-Minute Review: Good, Better, Best

Meeting #2: Troubleshoot/Pre-Mortem: Your responsibility is to address challenges remaining from the previous meeting and find solutions. If there are none, you'll conduct a "pre-mortem" to see where and how your project might fail. You have 12 minutes to accomplish this.

1-Minute Review: Good, Better, Best

Meeting #3: Finalize Our Jobs: Your responsibility is to finalize the assignments leading up to the launch of your project. You'll clarify who is to do what, how, and when. You can also use this meeting to design the next session (Sail the Plan). You have 12 minutes to accomplish this.

1-Minute Review: Good, Better, Best

LeadWell

Session #5: Examine the Holes   Meeting #1: Check In & Troubleshoot

Leader Meeting Instructions: Your responsibility is to lead your team in hearing progress reports on what has been done, including a discussion of facing challenges by noting them on a flip chart or whiteboard. You only have 12 minutes to accomplish this. Assign the Time Keeper and Scribe for this meeting. The Trainer will select two Responders for feedback.

Leader, read aloud: *This meeting is to help us be accountable by giving updates on the progress of each part of our plan. We'll try to problem-solve issues that come up. We have 12 minutes to accomplish this.*

Ideas:

- Restate the project and the goals of your leadership project.

- Refer to the flip chart/whiteboard items of the tasks that you've prepared beforehand. Let each leader/co-leader report on the progress.

- Discuss issues that need to be solved, changed, or revised.

- Review your accomplishments by stating the plan.

- Remember to thank everyone for their participation and announce that this portion of the meeting is now adjourned.

- Receive 1-minute feedback on your portion of meeting leading, and thank your Responders for the feedback.

LeadWell.

Session #5: Examine the Holes   Meeting # 2: Troubleshoot/Pre-Mortem

Leader Meeting Instructions: Your responsibility is to address challenges remaining from the previous meeting and find solutions. If there are none, you'll conduct a "pre-mortem" to see what might cause your project to fail. You only have 12 minutes to accomplish this. Assign the Time Keeper and Scribe for this meeting. The Trainer will select two Responders for feedback.

Leader, read aloud: *If the previous meeting revealed problems that need more time to fix, here is our goal: In this meeting we're going to continue to work on solving the problems that have come up from the last meeting.*

   If the previous meeting was completed without requiring further time to fix problems, here is our goal: *In this meeting we're going to do a pre-mortem, which will help us think about things that could go wrong in our project and then try to fix them. We have 12 minutes to accomplish this.*

Ideas:
- Restate the project and the goals of your leadership project.

- If you are doing the first goal, then refer to the flip chart/whiteboard items and see what else needs to be accomplished in this meeting.

- If you are doing the pre-mortem, here's what you do:
    - Say, "Let's imagine that our project failed. It was unsuccessful. We're going to pretend that we're analyzing why it failed and what caused the failure. "
    - Write on a flip chart/whiteboard reasons why the project failed.
    - Quickly determine which reasons seem the most logical, and then begin brainstorming ways to correct these in advance.
    - Make any changes to your current plans based on what you've thought about in this pre-mortem.

- Review your accomplishments. Remember to thank everyone for their participation.

- Receive 1-minute feedback on your portion of meeting leading, and thank your Responders for the feedback.

Session #5: Examine the Holes Meeting #3: Finalize Our Jobs

Leader Meeting Instructions: Your responsibility is to finalize the assignments leading up to the launch of your project. You'll clarify who is to do what, how, and when. You can also use this meeting to plan the next session (Sail the Plan). You only have 12 minutes to accomplish this. Assign the Time Keeper and Scribe for this meeting. The Trainer will select two Responders for feedback.

Leader, read aloud: *This meeting is to go over the plan details one more time and make sure that everyone understands his/her task, so we can prepare for (the event or the launch). We have 12 minutes to accomplish this.*

Ideas:

- Restate the project and the goals of your leadership project.

- Refer to the flip chart/whiteboard items and their timelines. Go over each, specifically addressing the leader/co-leaders and see if they have further issues to discuss.

- Review your accomplishments by stating the plan. Remember to thank everyone for their participation.

- Receive 1-minute feedback on your portion of meeting leading, and thank your Responders for the feedback.

The Trainer should summarize what happened in Session #5 and comment on how the four module concepts were involved. Then s/he will introduce what will take place in the next portion of this process, and announce the next Leaders (or however Session #6 is going to be structured).

Sail the Plan

Use this session to cover any final planning and troubleshooting needed or use it as the event or launch of the program you've been planning.

Key points:
- Option #1 is the project itself, whether it is an event or the launch of a program. Option #2 is an additional session to plan and troubleshoot problems in preparation for the project launch.
  - In option #1, you'll want to have someone assigned to record items in the log to prepare for your next session.
- Option #2, you'll want to invest the first part of the meeting to form the basis for the next.
  - In option #2, assign a Time Keeper and a Scribe to take notes in the meeting log.
  - Generally, the "Gel" method is recommended in this situation versus "Tell," "Sell," or "Del" style of leading.
  - At the end, provide a summary of the meeting results in order to help transition to the next meeting and/or session.

Option #1: Pre-Huddle, Event/Launch, Post-Huddle
Meeting #1: Pre-Huddle: One of the Co-Directors provides a final meeting to be sure that everyone understands his/her role and to give some inspiration as we go into the event. *1-Minute Review: Verbal-Written or Written*

Meeting #2: Event/Launch: Co-Directors provide guidance and supervision for the Leaders who are overseeing specific tasks for the event or program launch. *1-Minute Review: Verbal-Written or Written*
Meeting #3: Post-Huddle: One of the Co-Directors provides a wrap-up meeting to go over how things went and address any final issues as well as thanking the team members for their involvement. *1-Minute Review: Verbal-Written or Written*

Option #2: Event/Launch
Perhaps the first option just does not make sense for your Leadership Project. If not, then design this session with key assignments so Leaders understand their responsibilities and there are people assigned to record what happens and provide feedback.

Trainer may provide basic feedback, not to be confused with the final Session remaining. Trainer clarifies time and roles of next Session.

 **Lead**Well.

Session #6: Sail the Plan   Option #1

Meeting #1: Pre-Huddle Leader Instructions: One of the Co-Directors provides a final meeting to be sure that everyone understands his/her role and to give some inspiration as we go into the event.   *1-Minute Review: Verbal-Written or Written*

- You'll want to create your own meeting agenda for this huddle, based on your Leadership Project. Use elements from the previous meetings for ideas.

- Be sure there are appropriate people involved and that the Trainer is the Responder or has assigned Responders.

Meeting #2: Event/Launch: Co-Directors provide guidance and supervision for the Leaders who are overseeing specific tasks for the event or program launch. You may also want to plan this session per your situation and be sure someone is observing Leaders for feedback. *1-Minute Review: Verbal-Written or Written*

Meeting #3: Post-Huddle Leader Instructions: One of the Co-Directors provides a wrap-up meeting to go over how things went and address any final issues as well as thanking the team members for their involvement.
1-Minute Review: Verbal-Written or Written

- You'll want to create your own meeting agenda for this huddle, based on your Leadership Project. Use elements from the previous meetings for ideas.

- Be sure there are appropriate people involved and that the Trainer is the Responder or has assigned Responders.

Trainer may provide basic feedback, not to be confused with the final Session remaining. Trainer clarifies time and roles of next Session.

Session #6: Sail the Plan   Option #2 Event / Launch

Depending on what makes sense for your Leadership Project, you may want to design this more specifically to meet your needs. The primary purpose of this Session is the supervision of the event itself or the official launch of a program. Perhaps it is a school assembly where you announce a new policy. Maybe it's a big meeting or work day. Create a plan as to who is doing what if it differs from your existing plan, who'll provide feedback of leaders while they're leading, and who'll take notes on how things went so that you have reliable information for your final Session.

Notes:

Sift the Outcomes

This meeting is a time of reflection along with a celebration (or to plan a final celebration).

Key points:
- Restate what your project goal is from the log notes of the first SUCCESS session.
- Announce the results of the project.
- We'll be conducting three short meetings. The leader's responsibility is to keep us on track, monitor the time and group dynamics.
- Assign a Time Keeper and a Scribe to take notes in the meeting log.

Meeting #1: Post-Mortem: Your job is to lead a meeting where your team will analyze what went well and what didn't, and then try to uncover some of the reasons for both. You have 12 minutes to accomplish this.

1-Minute Review: Good, Better, Best

Meeting #2: Gleanings: Your job is to lead the team in a discussion on personal discoveries and what we learned through the process of leading this project. You'll also want to focus on the four concepts of this module. You have 12 minutes to accomplish this.

1-Minute Review: Good, Better, Best

Meeting #3: Celebration: Your job is to be the "Master of Ceremonies" for your party/celebration. If your team wants to have a separate celebration in order to thank people not on the leadership team, you'll be planning that in this meeting. You have 12 minutes to accomplish this.

1-Minute Review: Good, Better, Best

Session #7: Sift the Outcomes   Meeting #1: Post-Mortem

Leadership Meeting Instructions: Your job is to lead a meeting where your team will analyze what went well and what didn't, and then try to uncover some of the reasons for both. You only have 12 minutes to accomplish this. Assign the Time Keeper and Scribe for this meeting. The Trainer will select two Responders for feedback.

Leader, read aloud: *The goal of this meeting is for us to review what went well, what didn't go well, and why, and what we could improve on next time. We'll have 12 minutes to accomplish this.*

Ideas:

- Restate the project and the goals of your leadership project.

- Begin very generally in terms of how everything went as a whole. Let the team know you'll break it down in a moment.

- Consider writing these things on a flip chart or whiteboard:

- List three things that went well:
  - 1.
  - 2.
  - 3.

- List two things that didn't go well:
  - 1.
  - 2.

- Why didn't they go well?

- How did leaders respond to needed changes?

- What would you change next time for improvement?

- Review what you discussed.

- Receive 1-minute feedback on your portion of meeting leading, and thank your Responders for the feedback.

Session #7: Sift the Outcomes   Meeting #2: Gleanings

Meeting Leader Instructions: Your job is to lead the team in a discussion on personal discoveries and what we learned through the process of leading this project. You'll also want to focus on the four concepts of this module. You only have 12 minutes to accomplish this. Assign the Time Keeper and Scribe for this meeting. The Trainer will select two Responders for feedback.

Leader, read aloud: *Our last meeting in this session is about the project itself. In this meeting, we want to reflect on what we learned about leading, on a personal level and as a team. We'll be asking everyone to state at least one observation. We'll have 12 minutes to do this.*

Ideas:
- Consider having all the members take 1-2 minutes to reflect on and write down what they learned about their own leadership from this project. Writing focuses our thinking and helps us be more accountable. Then have everyone read what they wrote, and if interested, invite brief comments from others.
- Consider writing summary phrases on a whiteboard or flip chart to see if certain themes emerge.
- Ask for any other comments related to leading or examples, but again, keep the focus on leadership, not on the project itself.
- Ask the team to share on how these four concepts were seen throughout the project, and ask for specific illustrations if possible:
  - Team
  - Strategy
  - Servanthood
  - Responsibility

- Review highlights from the meeting. Remember to thank everyone for their participation.

- Receive 1-minute feedback on your portion of meeting leading, and thank your Responders for the feedback.

 **Lead**Well

Session #7: Sift the Outcomes   Meeting #3: Celebration

Leadership Meeting Instructions: Your job is to be the "Master of Ceremonies" for your party/celebration. If your team wants to have a separate celebration in order to thank people not on the leadership team, you'll be planning that in this meeting. You only have 12 minutes to accomplish this. Assign the Time Keeper and Scribe for this meeting. The Trainer will select two Responders for feedback.

Leader, read aloud: *The goal of our final meeting is* (select the appropriate one)
Option A: *To celebrate this project and completing the Emerald LeadWell Module.*
        Option B: *To plan a celebration for those involved in the project and completing the Emerald LeadWell Module.*

Option A: Exec Team Celebration: If this is your choice, hopefully you'll have some refreshments and personal affirmations of what people noticed others doing well. You may want to go around the circle and let everyone receive 3-4 positive comments on their leading and involvement in this module. Thank everyone for participating. The formal discussion and affirmations should take 12 minutes.

- Receive 1-minute feedback on your portion of meeting leading, and thank your Responders for the feedback.

Option B: Celebration Planning: Brainstorm a simple gathering for key people involved in making the project happen. This might include faculty, parents, other students, community leaders, etc. Discuss details as to time, location, refreshments, agenda, etc. Review the details and then thank everyone for their participation. This should take 12 minutes.

- Receive 1-minute feedback on your portion of meeting leading, and thank your Responders for the feedback.

Whatever option you select, the Trainer should summarize what happened and provide personal comments on the specific module concepts. The completion pins should be formally presented as well.

Leadership Project Report

Directions: Use this outline to prepare a report on what your team accomplished so we can share it with other young leaders around the world. Complete the online form at www.leadyoung.org or submit it by e-mail: info@kidlead.com. You can also post your photos and comments on the **Lead**Young Facebook link.

Name of Trainer:

Name of school/host organization, location/website:

- 20-30 word description of project:

- 40-50 word summary of how things went; the results:

- 40-50 word summary of what team members learned:

- Contact info for others if they have questions:

- Attach/upload photos.

For more info on how to send this report, contact us at info@kidlead.com

♔ Tips for Note Taking in the Project Log

Most of the time, when you're leading a meeting, you'll want to make your own notes and also assign someone to take the minutes, a role we're calling a "Scribe." Leaders need to realize that how the notes are written is important, because a person's notes can change the results of a meeting or how they are perceived by others. You want to be sure that notes are taken well, because you're going to be building off of previous meeting accomplishments. And you'll refer to the notes if there is a disagreement or if you need to hold people accountable.

The goal is to be thorough, but not wordy. Try to be specific, but focus on outcomes more than processes. Write so that a person not in the meeting could understand what happened and so that everyone present would say, "Yes, that's what took place." Include details such as topics discussed, names of people assigned duties, who was present (or absent), and the wording of motions made and specific votes. Finally, write so others can read it or have them word processed. In formal organizations, the minutes are legal documents. For this project, the log is an important communication tool.

Example of Not-So-Great Note Taking:
We had a good meeting. We talked more about what we should do. A lot of people shared their ideas. We are going to be planning a way to get the students to recycle in school. We came up with a lot of ideas and then decided which ones were the best.

Example of Clear Note Taking:
Jesse led us in a discussion of a brainstorm session on how to accomplish our goal, which is to launch a program to get our whole school to recycle. We came up with a lot of ideas, but the ones we decided on included:

- *Talking to the Principal to get the support of the staff (Co-Directors will do this and report in a week)*
- *Talk to Bristol High School to see how they launched their program (McKayla and Austin will do this and report in a week)*
- *Meeting with club presidents and student council for their ideas (Jesse will bring a list to the next meeting and then we'll assign team members to contact specific people and clubs)*

♔ Meeting Design Template

The SUCCESS Leader Project Plan is designed to provide sufficient structure, but still be flexible enough so leaders like you can accomplish unique goals. There may come times when you need to change or add a meeting in order to help you achieve your goal. If you need to do that, consider these ideas for designing your own meeting:

- **Time**: Strive to keep the objective achievable in 10-15 minutes, similar to the existing meetings.

- **Goal**: Clearly state the objective
    - Why is this needed as a change to the normal SUCCESS 7-step format?
    - Will this goal take you where you want to go?
    - Do you need any additional meetings to get where you need to go?
    - How will you measure the success of the meeting?

- **Assignments**: According to the SUCCESS format, who's going to be your Scribe, Time Keeper, and Responders who'll provide feedback?

⬤ Additional Leader Feedback Format

Leader running meeting: _____

How did this person do in leading the meeting? Put in a number for each question, based on this rating: 1-Could use improvement, 2-Fair, 3-Average, 4-Above Average, 5-Great

1. Ran the portion of the meeting efficiently (didn't waste time): _____

2. Listened to others' ideas: _____

3. Handled conflict and setbacks well: _____

4. Demonstrated responsibility in the task: _____

5. Communicated ideas clearly; spoke up: _____

6. Maintained a positive attitude: _____

7. Added significantly to this project: _____

8. Affirmed/honored others on the team: _____

9. Came up with good ideas; brainstormed well: _____

10. Displayed confidence; took charge when needed: _____

Comments:

LeadYoung. Training Systems © 2013, 2017, 2021 LeadWell Ruby Module
www.LeadYoungTraining.com

Experience all 4 Training Modules

Each module focuses on developing leadership skills via mini-project activities, the SUCCESS Leadership Project Plan, along with 4 of 16 essential leader qualities:

RUBY:
Sessions 1 & 2: Ethics (what it means to have high moral, internal standards)
Sessions 3 & 4: Honor (what it means to esteem people and value them)
Sessions 5 & 6: Communication (how to get your message to others)
Sessions 7 & 8: Power (how to get it and use it appropriately for good)

EMERALD:
Sessions 1 & 2: Responsible (what it means to be dependable, taking ownership)
Sessions 3 & 4: Servanthood (what it means to be humble and put the team first)
Sessions 5 & 6: Team (how to create unity and focus in your team)
Sessions 7 & 8: Strategy (how to get to the goal the best way)

GOLD:
Sessions 1 & 2: Commitment (what it means to be dedicated and persevere)
Sessions 3 & 4: Optimism (what it means to be hopeful in stressful situations)
Sessions 5 & 6: Conflict (how to diffuse potentially destructive emotions)
Sessions 7 & 8: Change (how to make transitions effectively)

SAPPHIRE:
Sessions 1 & 2: Integrity (what it means to be honest and internally whole)
Sessions 3 & 4: Confidence (what it means to exude faith, take risks)
Sessions 5 & 6: Recruit (how to get people on your team and in the right positions)
Sessions 7 & 8: Vision (how to decide direction and say it in a way that inspires others)

LeadYoung Training Systems © 2013, 2017, 2021 LeadWell Ruby Module
www.LeadYoungTraining.com

Resources

(Primarily designed for 19-23 year olds)

These 50 reproducible leader lessons empower you to train your colleagues and staff on a variety of practical leadership topics There is 1 page you can copy as a handout and 1 page with leader guides, including ideas for using them in 5- to 30-minute time slots. The last 5 lessons involve discussion guides for leader oriented movies to watch as a team. (8.5x11 inch format) Purchase at CreateSpace.com or Amazon.com.

This book shares essentials for effective leading in a narrative format, as a seasoned leader mentors a young leader. In addition to the story, there is a section on finding a leader mentor as well as being a mentor. This is a great book to be used between a mentor and protégé or a group of young leaders with discussion/reflection questions. Purchase at CreateSpace.com, Amazon.com or with bulk discounts at leadyoung.org.

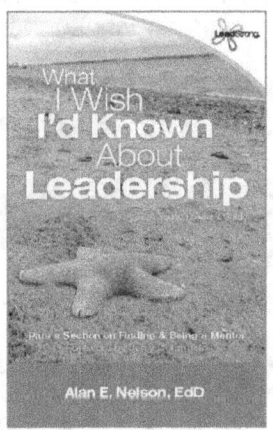

All leaders need to understand the secret of people, because they are in the people business. Although not specifically a book on leading, the principles in this narrative offer unique insights for emotional intelligence in the life of a leader. Leaders need to understand the importance of honor on a team and in an organization. There are leadership reflection/discussion questions in the back of the book. Purchase at CreateSpace.com, Amazon.com, or with bulk discounts at www.LeadYoungTraining.com.

Stage 1: *Ages 3-5* (KiddieLead)

A series of 16 full-color storybooks and the Green Module (only): includes Activity Training Manual (over 30 peer-led team projects). Find them on Amazon.com.

Stage 2: *Ages 5-9* (Lead1st)

Green, Red, Blue and Orange Modules and a storybook highlighting for each training manual. Each Activities Training Manual offers over 30 peer-led team projects. Purchase them on Amazon.com.

Stage 3: *Ages 10-13* (LeadNow)

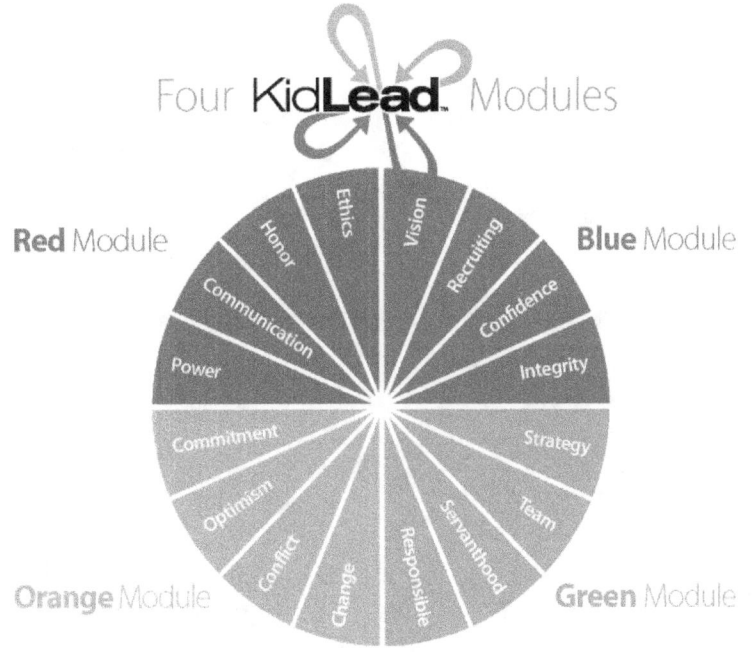

LeadYoung. Training Systems © 2013, 2017, 2021 LeadWell Ruby Module
www.LeadYoungTraining.com

www.ingramcontent.com/pod-product-compliance
Lightning Source LLC
Chambersburg PA
CBHW081241180526
45171CB00005B/502